Close that Sale!

A guide for consultative business to business sales

Michael Clingan

Close that Sale!

A guide for consultative business to business sales

Copyright © 2012 by Michael Clingan

Published by The Claymore Group, LLC

First Edition: March 2012

ISBN: 0615607519
ISBN-13: 978-0615607511

CONTENTS

ACKNOWLEDGMENTS

I'd like to thank my many sales and marketing teachers and influencers. They include a large number of Fortune's Global 500 and most of the major research institutions around the planet, former bosses like Dale Grant and Dennis Grannan, who had high expectations while giving me license to learn, amazing salespeople like Patrick Warholic and Victor Parziale, and the writings of two physicists on dialog, Eliyahu Goldratt and David Bohm.

I also wish to thank several of my consulting clients, Edward Hefter at Materion Electrofusion Products, Mary Louise Luczkowski at Biomed Diagnostics, April Sedano at PFI Tech, as well as David Fields of Ascendant Consulting for their unrelenting (and I chose that word carefully) encouragement to get the book done.

I thank Ellen Bryant of Ellen Bryant Design for producing a great book design and my other fellow coworkers at Cohere for sharing their expertise on matters of writing and social media.

And finally, I'd like to thank my wife, Stephanie, for her faith, patience and support, and our daughters Kelly and Meghan for keeping everything real and fun.

PREFACE

In the world of selling, having a professional conversation with a prospective buyer trumps making a great presentation to them. And being in a dialog, where shared meaning and mutual value are created, trumps having any other kind of conversation.

By "trumps" I mean "kicks its butt" as a way to close more and bigger orders.

I believe the ability to facilitate a dialog is the one skill that separates great salespeople from all the rest. At its worst, you build a foundation for future sales; at its best you become a full partner with your prospect in shaping and defining the entire sale.

But I'm not talking about just any kind of dialog. The dialog I'll describe is one designed to respectfully, but relentlessly, advance a sale until it is closed.

This book is unique in that I didn't write it by building upon ideas from other sales books or by adding a new acronym to the sales lexicon. Instead, I'll detail an approach that I adapted from outside the world of sales — from an amazing class I took on gaining buy-in for major organizational change.

While I was attending that class it occurred to me that the organizational change cases we were studying, where the stakes are very high, and yet where there is often little motivation for change, are the world's toughest consultative sales. If an approach worked there, it could work with prospective customers.

And it does.

FORWARD

Like many of you, I too became an accidental salesperson. In my case, the phone was ringing in the sales office, and due to some unplanned turnover, no one was there to answer it. I picked it up and found myself talking with a real live sales prospect.

As a product engineer I knew our specs and features, but for some reason I didn't start telling the caller (my first prospect!) all of that "stuff" — instead I asked about their needs and how they intended to use the product.

I took notes, asked more questions, summarized what I'd heard, and committed to sending a customized quotation that afternoon with a phone call to follow. It would end up being a $25,000 sale of our specialized scientific instrumentation.

After hanging up I realized our CEO was standing in the doorway. He said, "I think you're our new sales manager." It took some work, but after he sold me on sales as a career move I asked him about my new goals. He responded, "40% growth would be great." Not knowing any better I said, "Ok."

That 40% growth goal became my annual "boogie" for the next five years. I made it four out of those five years, mainly due to an insane amount of work and adopting new selling models as we grew. The other year I came in at 39.5%, which sounds good, but in sales, and particularly in our environment, was still an embarrassing miss. I made sure it was my only one.

My sales career moved on to large system sales, electrical components, and finally to technical and educational services. Along the way I've had titles like National Sales Manager, Worldwide Director of Sales and Marketing, and VP of Sales. It's been my pleasure to hire, develop, manage, and lead numerous sales and sales rep teams full of great people.

The fact that I've had only one miss is due to three things:

1. My first sale convinced me that prospects know a lot about what they need and that asking the right questions, without letting my ego get in the way, is a key to consultative sales success.

2. I was usually the underdog; working for foreign companies in new markets, startups, or turnarounds. I found I'd lose if I played like everyone else, so I didn't and I still don't.

3. I became a student of sales and marketing: taking classes and reading two or three books every month, trying out what I'd read, and keeping only what worked. I initially hated closing, so I was particularly interested in learning to close a consultative sale in a way that clients appreciated.

This book is focused on this last point: consultative closing. My goal is to help you, the professional salesperson, the executive, the consultant, or the freelancer, to close your consultative sales opportunities more effectively, without stress, and in a way that can truly transform your relationships with prospects and customers.

I hope this book makes your list of "keepers." I also hope that we meet in a class or presentation someday, and that you are wildly successful as a respected, high value, consultative closer.

Michael Clingan
Loveland, Colorado
michael@transformativeselling.com

INTRODUCTION

This book was written for the professional salesperson as well as the person who wants to sell like a professional.

If you're in the second category, you may have found that when you became a business owner, consultant, entrepreneur, or freelancer, you also became the lead salesperson for your product, service or ideas.

To some readers, sales may have seemed a little scary or even a bit unethical, which is a common misperception people have about the job of a salesperson. Luckily, neither are the case — I've found sales to be both exciting and fulfilling, and practicing ethical behavior is the key to ongoing sales success.

This book was written to help you improve your skills in closing a consultative sale more often, for more money, and at higher margins. This is done by facilitating a closing focused sales dialog specifically designed around how prospects make decisions.

Before we get started, I want to state that I will not be referring to this dialog as a sales process. Here's why:

The first sales process was diagramed in 1887 by John Patterson, the CEO of NCR, to better sell cash registers. Things are a little more complicated now; I recently Googled "sales process" and got 54 million hits with 9.5 million sales process diagrams.

With numbers like that, you'd think we would have developed a lot of different takes on how to sell something in the last one-hundred and twenty plus years. As it turns out, when you strip away the fluff, the consultative sales process is almost always described or diagramed the same way — as a sequence of activity boxes or steps to be checked off, usually something along the lines of:

❑ Step One: Qualifying

❑ Step Two: Building rapport

❑ Step Three: Discovering needs

❑ Step Four: Presenting the solution

❑ Step Five: Overcoming objections

❑ Step Six: Closing the deal

These steps, done one after the other, describe how we are usually taught to sell. They are tried and true, but only true enough to work consistently in entry level and very static consultative sales situations. They are but nuanced versions of the way you'd sell in a transactional sales environment — a place we'll talk about in a few pages, but one very different from what we find in consultative selling.

There are problems with each of these sales process steps, but steps five and six, where the salesperson moves into persuasion mode, are exactly where most of the negative perceptions about sales arise, as the salesperson begins to push and the prospect naturally begins to resist.

None of these steps reflect the reality of how a consultative sale is closed in the mind of the prospect. They may answer the question of "What are you doing on the account?" but not

"Where is the prospect in their decision making?" and "What can I do to help them?"

To answer these last questions, I suggest your forget following a process of checkboxes and instead engage your prospect in a dialog specifically designed to help them focus, gain clarity, and move naturally from one small decision to the next until they demonstrate they're ready to start by placing the order.

The Closing Dialog

This dialog is designed so that you can guide your prospect through the five "stages" of decision making while you attend to the three surrounding "states" of closing management.

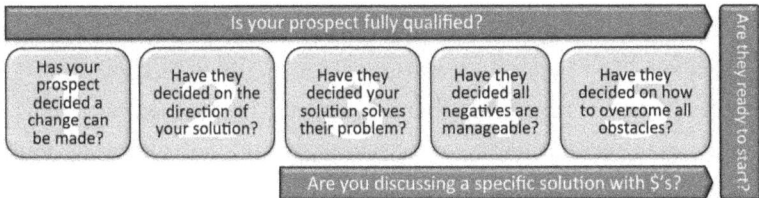

I use the term "stages" instead of "steps" because, when asked if a "step" has been made or achieved, it is too easy for a salesperson to respond "yes" if they've taken an action. Using the term "stages" is a reminder to the salesperson to consider the prospect's real-life decision making status.

The five stages begin with a prospect being open to making a decision and end with their agreement as to how and when a valuable and desirable solution can be safely and efficiently implemented.

Meanwhile, the three states guide your account management actions through the dialog.

It's important to remember that these stages and states are facilitated by the salesperson, but the pace of the dialog is determined by the prospect. If the prospect feels they are being pushed too hard to make a decision too fast, the dialog will break down.

This lack of pace control may feel frustrating to some salespeople but, in my experience, the total time spent in a dialog is less than the total time required to close without one. There is usually far less need recover the same points in a dialog and far less time dealing with last minute problems.

As always, the salesperson remains completely responsible for discovery, analysis, and proposal preparations and presentations throughout the dialog — the "consulting" part of consultative sales.

You've probably noticed that two classic sales process steps, qualifying and presenting (commonly thought of as discrete events) aren't represented that way in our dialog roadmap. This is because they can be very transient aspects of a sale in the real world.

For example, a prospect can be fully qualified, then the deal evolves in some direction where they don't have sufficient authority or budget to make a decision; now they're no longer qualified. The deal can evolve again, and the prospect may be back to being qualified.

If a prospect becomes unqualified, the salesperson needs to expand the sale to include whoever is needed to return the sale to a "qualified" state.

"Presenting" faces a similar challenge. The prospect's needs and environment are likely to change between discovery and the close. The presentation often takes on new dimensions as it may serve as a portfolio of possible solution scenarios, only one or two of which are being actively considered.

I suggest that we recognize these realities and view the "decider," our specific solution, and its ROI, all as evolving states. We can then incorporate that perspective and our flexibility around those states into the dialog. This will make us far more responsive than our competition and give us a better chance to steer the sale.

In fact, you may have already sensed these problems with qualifying and presenting as you manage your sales pipeline or funnel. They show up as a bottleneck just after Step Four in the list of typical sales process checkboxes: It's very difficult to overcome objections to what has become the wrong deal or to close someone who is no longer the right person.

By the way, any sales management pipeline or forecasting tools that you might use can be adapted to the approach used in this book. If you do this, and if you're factoring (weighting) your forecast, there is a key inflection point when the probability of a sale goes way up. I'll highlight that point when we get to it.

In the following pages I'll highlight how a structured but natural dialog provides a far better way of closing the highest possible value deals for both you and your prospects.

Or, simply put, being in a sales dialog trumps being in a sales conversation. And yeah, I really mean "kicks its butt."

1 THE SALES LANDSCAPE

There are so many different methods and terms used in sales that I think a "reboot" would be a good idea before introducing a new way to close. This will also benefit the non-sales professionals who are reading this book. In this reboot I'll discuss selling, closing, transitional and consultative sales, and some of the special challenges in closing the consultative sale.

Let's begin with two useful definitions:

Selling is influencing someone to make a decision to buy from you instead of either using another resource or doing nothing.

Closing is the act of actively receiving a firm and specific order while selling.

Selling without closing is just having a chat or doing a presentation, it can feel great — it's just not something that's going to generate many orders.

It is the ability to close that makes a salesperson a salesperson. This ability can be learned or dramatically improved with training and practice.

Transactional Selling

In a transactional sales opportunity, the prospect is making a buying decision based primarily on price and features, and they're often making that decision rather quickly. In fact, the salesperson and the prospect may meet only once. This can put incredible pressure on the salesperson to immediately try and close the transaction before that meeting ends. Often times, a salesperson feels so much pressure that many of the negative behaviors and manipulative closing tactics associated with sales and selling occur as a direct result of this intense need to close fast.

These tactics include such-well known staples as the Puppy Dog close, the Franklin T close, the Alternative Choice close and the Takeaway close. Other closing tactics can be more subtle but are usually based on manipulating some type or level of fear.

A classic example of transactional selling can be found by taking a trip to buy a new flat screen TV:

You walk into a "big box" store and head to the television area. Rows of flat screens are showing the same scene from the movie *Inception*, the one where the horizon rolls up into the sky.

As you search for models in your budget with the features you want, a salesperson walks over to help you. They talk to you about sizes, brands, and features and help you narrow your choice down to one or two models. They point out a feature or two that the lower-priced model is lacking.

The salesperson knows that you're either going to buy now, that you'll leave and go to another store, or that you may not buy anything at all. They also know that you'll probably be checking for better prices on your iPhone while you're standing there, and that it's unlikely they'll see you again when you leave the store.

So, the salesperson makes a point of telling you that the store has a 30-day free return policy ("try it you'll like it", a form of the Puppy Dog close) or that the particular model you're looking at is likely to be discontinued or will have a price increase soon (the Takeaway) or they may ask if you want help loading it or would rather it be delivered and installed (the Alternative close.)

You buy or you walk.

Transactional selling also takes place in the business-to-business (B2B) world: A salesperson calls a prospect or responds to an inquiry with features, pricing, and delivery information. Then, in some manner, they try to close the order.

If they do most of the above while sitting in their own cubical or office they're called internal salespeople; if they do it in a prospect's cubical or office they're usually called field sales. If they call on the same prospect over time they're often referred to as being in "relationship" sales, as they're expected to build a relationship with prospective buyers.

I have a fundamental problem with B2B transactional sales: Anything that can be sold, routinely and successfully, in a transactional manner is a commodity. Beyond price and features, commodities are differentiated in the business-to-consumer (B2C) markets by promises of better quality, delivery, or consistency of product or service. However, in the B2B world, all of these attributes are pretty much assumed in the mind of the buyer. So much so that I joke that B2B buyers are looking for free, perfect, and now, which really isn't much of a joke when you're the salesperson on the account.

I'll also warn that in the B2B transactional sales game, salespeople spend a great deal of time fighting with their own operations people and worrying about protecting increasingly narrow margins. It's a tough game without many opportunities for sales creativity.

As for relationship selling, most buyers are looking for relationships that bring value and not just familiarity. Knowing their kid's name is nice, but helping their business in a measurable way is the real name of the game.

Consultative Selling

In a consultative sales opportunity, the prospect is, along with initial price, considering the cost (as in startup cost, total cost of ownership, lifetime cost, or even net present value) and the benefits of competing products or services. The buying cycle is usually in the range of weeks to months, and there is a real possibility of a long-term business relationship between individual buyers and sellers.

A strategic sales opportunity is a special type of consultative sale that is usually conducted at the enterprise level where the prospect is interested in creating new directions for their business or in dramatically growing or improving their business. The buying cycle is in the months to years range, and the prospect and the successful seller often form a longer-term partnership lasting through several projects or even years. A strategic opportunity may begin as a consultative one.

Both consultative and strategic sales opportunities require a consultative selling approach. This is because both situations require the salesperson to discover needs, create and analyze options, and present a solution. This is identical to a consultant's approach with a client and the "consultative" name has been adopted to reflect the salesperson's very similar approach with a prospect.

Consultative selling is done by professional salespeople, executives who support sales in the field, business consultants, small business owners, trainers, speakers, and freelancers of all kinds.

The "consultative" part of consultative selling may be as simple as asking questions to help a prospect choose from various standard options to configure a product or service. It can also be as complex as conducting a deep and professional assessment of the prospect's situation and creating a completely custom or even a radically new solution to meet their needs.

Additional hallmarks of consultative selling include:

A deeper and richer interaction, usually over a period of time, between the salesperson and the prospect.

The role of the salesperson in understanding the current and desired states of the prospect's situation and in developing a clear path from the former to the later.

At the end of the day, the "sales" part of consultative selling is the same as in all sales. The salesperson must help the prospect become a customer. In other words, they must "close them.".

Challenges In Consultative Closing

There are several common issues faced by many consultative salespeople. I'd like to touch on six:

1. Closing can be an extremely uncomfortable situation for many salespeople. Asking for a commitment is seen as a good way to be rejected, to have one's work and goals dashed, and for the sales opportunity to go away.

2. The "deeper and richer interaction" level of the consultative sale sometimes results in the prospect seeing the salesperson as an advisor and the salesperson seeing the prospect as someone they're mentoring, and possibly even as a friend. Toss in a bit of a lingering perception from negative transactional sales experiences that sales success requires manipulation, and you end up with a salesperson that will take an order from a friend, but they would never try to close them, as that would require "manipulation" and friends simply don't manipulate friends.

3. Many consultative salespeople focus primarily on the "consultative" part, thinking or hoping that if they do a good enough job consulting, the prospect will see their value and they'll win the sale. It seldom seems to work out that way. All too often the consulting-focused salesperson ends up educating their prospect to be a better buyer from a competitor or to implement a solution on their own.

These three are all examples of "closing reluctance," the counterpoint to "call reluctance" where a salesperson is hesitant to initiate a first meeting.

You will see that my sales dialog has been designed to avoid closing reluctance by building naturally from one easier decision to the next, by moving much of the "action" decisions forward to remove closing stress, and by having the salesperson and the prospect almost exchange sides of the table along the way.

4. Another problem I commonly see is an unwillingness to really probe the prospect's pain, and importantly, the possible pain from the salesperson's own solution

before asking for the order. Failing to do both tells the prospect to beware: "Shallow solution ahead and good luck making it work."

5. In a typical sales process, closing follows a presentation, which follows a statement of need. This sequence serves us poorly, as the prospect's needs can evolve throughout the consultative sale — while there is an initial need, provided either by the prospect or the salesperson, after doing the work of discovery, additional layers of needs are often revealed along the way.

6. Closing is often the end of a discussion, which after going here and there, winds down to an uncomfortable pause, aka "The Big Closing Moment." This creates way too much pressure on both the buyer and the seller.

I'll discuss how to facilitate a sales dialog that progresses in the same way a prospect naturally makes a decision, building with greater clarity and safety until it's a simple matter of agreeing when to start. It's usually something of an anticlimactic closing moment. But I'll take it!

I've personally used the following sales dialog to close across numerous industries, organizational levels, and international cultures. I'll present each stage and state in the order in which you would normally facilitate them, as you advance the closing dialog.

Let's begin with a concept that can help keep you on track from "soup to nuts."

2 STAY QUALIFIED

Qualifying is the act of determining if someone is a real prospect for your service or product. Here are three great reasons to qualify:

1. Consultative selling is really hard work. It requires configuring a standard set of solutions or products, or the creation of a custom solution or product to meet your prospect's needs. The "inside your own company" sales work to support such an offer can be even harder than the external work with the prospect. Make sure your prospect can buy from you before doing that work by qualifying them.

2. By qualifying you'll also reduce the stress levels, for both you and the prospect, as the reasons for the sales dialog will have been well established.

3. The qualification process provides a solid foundation for everything that comes afterward, including that magic moment when the prospect becomes a customer.

A qualified prospect has three attributes — money to spend, authority to spend it, and a need to address. Two out of three won't do, all three qualifying attributes are required to close.

Some parse the need component into need and time. I've never seen a benefit from doing this: if the need isn't pressing, as either pain or opportunity, it isn't much of a need.

Here's where we're at on our map:

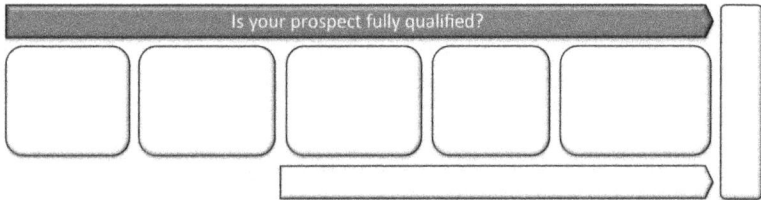

Helping a prospect fix a lacking attribute should be your first priority as a salesperson, if, and this is important, you decide to sell to them at all at this time. If you have more qualified prospects, your time will likely be better rewarded by selling to those prospects first.

As I mention, to be fully qualified to make the buying decision, a prospect must have the money, the authority, and a need. The acronym "MAN" is an easy way to remember these three attributes.

Money: Verify the budget available for a particular need. That doesn't mean you'll need to constrain your solution against that budget but you'll have an idea of what you're selling against. In consultative selling, it is very easy to sell to the solution that you, as an expert, know the prospect needs instead of selling them something priced at what they want to spend.

Authority: Identify who is making the buying decision. It may be your prospect, it might be their boss, or it might be a committee. Better to know and bring these people into the selling dialog as early as possible. Otherwise you'll be asking your prospect to sell to someone else for you. That usually doesn't go as well as we'd wish.

Need: In consultative selling the need is the prospect's problem. It's why they're talking with you. Either they come to you with a need or you go to them because you suspect (or even know) they have a need. Without an identified need your job is a lot harder.

Now for the really challenging part: As your dialog with the prospect progresses, the scope, resources, pricing, timing, and many other details will likely change, sometimes so much that your prospect is no longer the decision maker or at least not the only one.

When I was selling to Nokia mobile phones, I asked for and received a diagram showing how buying decisions were made and who, exactly, had authority to do what. The diagram had a series of labeled concentric circles on it. It was clear, authoritative, and completely wrong. I found that, in reality, Nokia used a complicated approval matrix where there was a sourcing (new program purchasing) authority over each model, each platform (such as CDMA or GSM), and each region where the phone was to be built. However, no one person was entirely responsible for all three aspects. As their plans to manufacture a phone changed, so too did my qualification strategy.

Keep checking that the prospect is still qualified for the deal as the deal evolves. Many times a prospect <u>was</u> qualified, but the dialog has broadened the needed solution or even taken it in a completely new direction. You're now trying to close someone that has realized they can't make a commitment to the deal. That's frustrating for both of you.

To avoid that frustration, periodically re-qualify your prospect with questions such as the following:

1. "If we were to move ahead right now, would you be the project owner?"

2. "Who would be surprised to see this project starting up in its current configuration?

3. "Just checking to see if this is still in your budget as we've got a better picture now of what's needed."

4. "Who else benefits from this project?"

5. "What other funds or resources would we need to make this work? Who controls them?"

Qualification is not a step to be checked off, it's an ongoing process.

3 SMALL DECISIONS, BIG ORDERS

There is usually a greater risk and no offsetting benefit to asking your prospect to make a huge leap of a decision when several smaller "baby steps" will do. The challenge for the consultative closer is to sequence and directly connect each of those smaller decision stages to the next so that they lead to a closed sale.

Your best bet is to make the decision-making process a natural dialog for your prospects, with small decision checkpoints along the way, and you'll close more sales. Surprisingly, you'll probably also make those sales more quickly.

This is how to start that dialog: Instead of jumping into the presentation of a solution and then asking for a big decision or for a contract, the first point of discussion would be to help the prospect simply agree that a choice or decision can be made. Yes, this seems to be an absurdly small decision but it is highly effective as it nudges the prospect into motion and creates momentum.

I also suggest that you view the prospect's participation at this early point as something of a fourth qualifying attribute — the willingness to make a small first decision portends their willingness to make the last one.

If the prospective buyer has come to you, this first small decision has already been made: otherwise, your first task is to establish either that there are problems of some kind with the current situation or that solution options exist to known problems.

To do this:

1. Ask relevant situational questions about their business, performance, processes, customer complaints, employee turnover, or about your own area of potential value.

2. Ask questions about the actions they've taken around the above situations in the past.

3. Don't try to be an expert (yet): your role is to ask probing and intelligent questions in a respectful way.

4. Once the topic is opened an inquisitive "Really?" or two is all that is usually needed to progress the dialog. Avoid throwing out solutions at this stage, as you may want to charge for them later.

5. Once your prospect has made the case for you that a decision can be made, summarize and ask for their agreement on this point.

A series of small decisions that lead to a close is better than trying or hoping for a single big decision.

4 THE DIRECTION OF THE SOLUTION

Here is the next small decision stage for your prospect: It's a subtle and yet powerful move you can take before talking about the details of your particular solution. Simply discuss and help your prospect decide on the general type or nature of the solution that will solve their problem.

Doing this serves two purposes: It rules out lots of competition and brings focus to what you'll be proposing.

In chess, this kind of move is called "zwischenzug" or "intermezzo." It's the surprise move a master makes in the middle of a series of expected moves and it's the move that makes all the difference in the result of the game.

Don't underestimate the power of such a quiet little move! Most sales prospects are resigned to enduring a sales pitch and then having to reorient the salesperson a few times toward what they see to be the solution to their problem. Instead of a pitch, ask the prospect to describe what the solution might look like. If their answer is aligned with where you're taking them, you're done. If they're not aligned, you have some work to do.

Sometimes a prospect has a hard time getting past the irritating or costly symptoms of their problem to understanding what type of solution is needed. An approach that can help here is the "Five Why's." This tool originated in the Toyota Production System and is normally used to identify the root cause of a process problem, but it can work great in sales.

It's easy to use the Five Why's: Ask the prospect why the problem exists. They'll give you a reason. Accept that reason and ask why that reason exists. Sometimes I just say, "Really?" or "Why do you think that is?" in an inquisitive way. They'll go deeper and give you another reason. You take that reason and ask again "Why?" or words to that effect.

Be careful not to be annoying, just politely inquisitive. Listen carefully to their answers, make sure they're clear to you, and don't judge them. Judging disrupts the dialog and makes it appear you're questioning their ability to do their job. Don't do that.

The goal of asking the same question, "Why?", over and over is simple: to get beyond symptoms and closer to the cause of your prospect's potential area of pain.

Use as many of the Five Why's as you need, stopping when you can rephrase their last answer and express it as the direction of your solution.

Please be aware that if you can't find a "Why" for your solution, there probably isn't a sale to be made for you on this particular problem. You can backup and look for another problem, provide the prospect with a valuable referral to another resource, or respectfully disengage from the sales process.

Of course you may already have in mind a direction for the solution. It could be a standard thing you sell, what you just sold to someone else, or it might be the result of your insight, intuition, and industry knowledge. But having your prospect suggest the direction first will be invaluable in closing the order.

Questions to ask:

4. Use the Five Whys to gain a deeper understanding of the problem.

5. "What do you think the root cause of this problem is?"

6. "What is the general thinking on this?"

7. "In a perfect world, how would things work?" You can then work backwards from that endpoint through the solution – this is what consultants do to scope a project.

8. "What are the one or two biggest things keeping your team from being more productive or profitable right now?"

Encourage your prospect to describe how they see the solution working at its best. **Reach agreement on the direction of the solution before moving ahead.**

5 GET SPECIFIC AND STAY THERE

The next small decision stage you'll want the prospect to reach is that there is a specific solution available that will solve their problem.

At a high level, there are three urgent reasons to make a buying decision: The burning platform, a way to avoid pain, and the chance to seize an opportunity.

1. A burning platform is a looming "disaster" such as a change in government regulations, a new technology dramatically shifting their playing field, or a major adjustment in their industry or customer base.

2. The pain they might avoid includes unnecessary cost, hassle, uncertainty, or risk and extreme competitive pressures.

3. Opportunities include the chance to expand markets, retain customers, or improve efficiencies.

Of the three, I least prefer selling to a common pain (the middle one) for several reasons: First, these are usually complex sales that involve numerous people, where only one, two or even none of whom may have the authority to make a "go" decision. Second, the organization has already developed "work arounds" around most pain in the form of policies, procedures, or even whole departments whose job is to mitigate a certain kind of pain. As a result, your solution, no matter how elegant, could be seen as difficult to implement or even as disruptive.

Ask questions to help the prospect feel the heat on the platform, the all too familiar and often chronic pain or the sweetness of the opportunity. Once you have a general picture of the situation begin helping your prospect specify exactly what they want to change. This dialog can begin with a "what if…" or a "in a perfect world." Whenever a number, goal, metric, or defined state of being is mentioned, write it down. Use these notes to describe a specific desired end state (the result of a service performed or a product delivered and installed) for your prospect. Ask them to confirm that this is exactly what they want as their desired end state.

There is a huge upside to driving this dialog more capably, and getting more specific, than your competitors.

An example of this was when one of my salespeople was selling to a major research institution. Our competition was a company with a great off-the-shelf product, a decade long relationship with the senior decision maker, and they were offering a large discount. My salesperson had already moved the opportunity down to less than a 25% chance of a win on her forecast.

Our only real chance was to change what was being bought. We began a conversation with the other two decision makers, asking open-ended questions as to where they planned to take their research and what future challenges they foresaw from an equipment standpoint. As it turned out, their goal was to have both cutting edge and a very versatile set of core capabilities. These would run well over a million dollars — far beyond what the other decision maker was interested in.

We also found that the two junior researchers had submitted a grant proposal that, if funded in the next fiscal year, could pay for everything they wanted. No one, however, knew the odds of the grant being funded, particularly as one of the researchers was in his first year at the institution.

Moving very quickly, we configured a solution with three unique components: First, a solid and basic equipment setup that had a key expansion capability that would support the junior researcher's vision. Second, the loan, available only through us, of next generation equipment from a UK-based firm wanting to get into the US market that took advantage of our key expansion capability. And third, no discount but rather a grant designed to trigger matching funds from the US government — together totaling more than our competition's discount.

If the prospect's grant came through, they'd be obligated to buy all of the equipment, if not the UK firm would at least have a well- known reference customer in the US. They'd even be able to use the installation for periodic product demonstrations.

The prospect's purchasing department called me a couple of times with a few questions, and when the RFP came out we were sole sourced, as they now knew precisely what they wanted and we could get them get there in a way no one else could match.

The junior researchers ended up getting their grant, so it turned out to be over a million dollar order. They then bought another $250k of accessories from us the following year at list price. That was a nice bonus.

We'd changed the playing field on one sales call by helping the prospects specify all of their needs more precisely than our competition.

I've used this approach numerous times, and it always does two wonderful things for me: It gives me an exact cost of my solution for ROI and pricing, and it allows me to far better differentiate my offer. Once I have a super-specific need and solution I do my best to accelerate the remainder of the purchasing process to avoid risk of circling back to competing on price for the order.

Questions you might ask:

1. Do you mind spending just a few minutes to make sure we've got our configuration together?

2. Test the "edges" to see what the prospect perceives as being "in" or "out" of the deal.

3. Will this solution make everyone happy, or are we missing something?

Help your prospect to see, and keep seeing, your precise solution.

6 ARE YOU SOLVING THEIR PROBLEM?

Now is the time to ask for a small but vital decision to be made by your prospect: Does the general solution you're discussing look like it can potentially solve their problem?

Is your prospect fully qualified?				
Has your prospect decided a change can be made?	Have they decided on the direction of your solution?	Have they decided your solution solves their problem?		
		Are you discussing a specific solution?		

This decision is a checkpoint, but it is not their final answer.

It is common in sales to try to rush the prospect along as quickly as possible from the first "yes" to a signature. While that can work, a prospect's natural reaction, when pushed, is to push back.

This is one of those times to go slow in order to go fast.

Take a few minutes to be sure your prospect thinks you're doing something important together. Your prospect will appreciate it, they won't feel pressured, and you won't waste your time and energy advancing the sale of something right up until when it just won't close.

7 PUT A PRICE TAG ON THE PROBLEM

There's another aspect to having a specific solution, it's having the dollar figures to accompany that solution. These dollar figures should include not only the price but also the agreed ROI expected. I suggest having specific dollar amounts for any deal configuration you've discussed.

As documented by Neil Rackham in his classic book, *SPIN Selling*, this alone will dramatically increase your closing rate. Besides, if you want to sell your value as a consultant, you need to establish, what that value is with your prospect.

To do this, after you and your prospect have agreed on a specific solution, work together to quantify its value. If they say something takes four hours every week, ask for a dollar value for that time.

If they're having a problem with a dollar figure, suggest one you've researched, cite your source, and then ask the prospect to confirm that your number is close. If their turnover is high, ask them what it cost to recruit and train a new employee and to estimate lost productivity in the interim. Then, multiply that by the number of employees they've lost. If they say they may lose 12% of a certain market, ask what the dollar impact will be for that loss.

While the solution should be specific, an approximation or estimate on the dollar amount is good enough. If you're not providing a serious multiplier of their current cost as an ROI due to your solution, you're probably not in the game anyway.

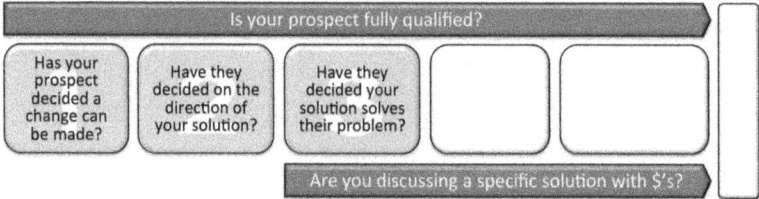

Is your prospect fully qualified?				
Has your prospect decided a change can be made?	Have they decided on the direction of your solution?	Have they decided your solution solves their problem?		
	Are you discussing a specific solution with $'s?			

Sometimes a prospect, even in a high level consultative sales situation, will regress to transactional buying behaviors. They'll usually return to price as the decision criteria because they don't trust their own total cost estimates. Now is the time to reinforce your solution's value by reviewing and agreeing (again) upon the total cost, benefits, and opportunities to be created.

Remember to ask about lost opportunities as well. What is the cost of a new product's development project taking another quarter (projects always seem to slip by quarters)?

The magnitude or total impact of these dollar estimates can be surprisingly high:

Let's say you're proposing a new sales forecasting or distribution management system. Either of these could greatly reduce your prospect's need to hold a high level of finished goods inventory. As it turns out, finished goods inventory holding cost are typically estimated to be in the 18 to 25% per year range, meaning every five million in extra inventory is costing your prospect about a million dollars a year. It's as if they were buying their inventory with a high-rate credit card, but without earning any points or miles. This is one number you'd use to calculate your solution's ROI.

Or, if you were proposing an employee retention solution, ROI factors would include costs related to employee turnover. Recruiting, hiring, and on-boarding costs are usually well quantified. Overtime, peer stress and opportunity cost are usually not quantified as well, so be sure to estimate and include them. In sales it may take a new salesperson six months after hire, product training, and orientation to begin contributing — as in making their first sale for their new company. What's the total cost then of losing and replacing a salesperson? It could easily be a couple of million dollars in lost revenue, plus recruitment cost of one-third of the first year's on-target-earnings and another half of a year's salary for the new salesperson as they come up to speed.

Costs such as these are often ignored, absorbed into various operational areas or otherwise hidden. It's your job as a salesperson to make them visible. Use big flashing lights if need be! All of these costs are the starting point of your value calculation. The other part is, of course, your price.

(A quick aside: I don't believe in discounting — that's a transactional sales game. I do believe in selling at high margins supported by superior value to a customer.)

Know the typical value for your solution before you ask the prospect for the cost of their problem. Help them, if need be, to understand all the cost components. Information resources include industry as well as professional organizations, the financial press, and academic research papers. I also use Linkedin Groups. Many times the answers you're looking for have already been discussed. Other times you may need to join the group and post your question.

I learned the hard way to look at value from every possible perspective (as my prospect might have) and not just the ones in my own pricing model.

Years ago I was assigned what can only be called a "sales mission" to become a supplier to Ford within sixty days. Normally this could take years but we needed to rapidly boost the perceived value of our company for a potential merger with a company who supplied the European automotive market.

With some research I found a current Ford supplier that used parts like ours, but made theirs in-house.

I got an appointment and flew to meet them, intending to fly back that night. As preparation I'd had our engineers put together some samples (one from a washing machine — hey, it's what I had) and I'd also done detailed costing estimates based on a variety of labor rates.

I met with several purchasing and engineering folks, some of whom unfortunately remembered an earlier, and poorer quality, incarnation of our company. I can laugh now, but the first question their lead purchaser asked was "You're not the same company that used to send us nothing but crap are you?" Once we got past that we were able to discuss Ford's quality requirements and our manufacturing processes in some detail. Things ended up in a good place and they asked me to come back for another meeting with a VP the next morning.

When I walked into the meeting room it was packed with fifteen or so people who were already suffering from a lack of oxygen. We started by rehashing what we'd covered the day before, then the VP moved directly to asking about our pricing.

I responded by asking about their fully burdened labor rate, a question he wouldn't answer. So I suggested a rate I'd found in my research for an area near their factory (it was in another state). He said that was very close. I then played my card: I suggested a number for their current finished part cost to the thousandth of a cent. He got a strange look, called for a printout, and then grilled me for at least five minutes on how I'd gotten my information. It wasn't fun but I knew I'd nailed it and that I could price aggressively with a high margin and still save them money.

I wanted to start quickly but they responded that Ford would have to qualify our parts, which would take 6 months to a year. I'd already confirmed that they were in a savings sharing plan with Ford so I suggested that we offer some of the savings immediately to Ford if they'd fast track our approval, which is what happened.

All of this sounds good doesn't it? Here's what I didn't know at the time — and it's the two reasons I got those meetings so fast and two things I wished I'd factored in to my pricing and sales approach: One, Ford had been rejecting, in increasing numbers, some of their parts and two, they'd had three carpal tunnel syndrome settlements on their out-of-state production lines used for the Ford parts.

My research on cost, as good as it was, didn't reveal that they were in danger of losing the Ford business or include all the dollars they were paying in settlements. While neither was something a prospect would brag about, I learned then to ask a broader range of probing questions, including those related to quality, safety, and HR aspects of the decision making process and ROI calculations.

For many types of solutions it's often better to use net profit, contribution or margin dollars instead of gross sales so that the prospect can more directly calculate your solution's impact.

The dollars associated with each specific solution being discussed should include the buyer's investment as well as the direct and indirect cost of their current pain or their missed opportunity.

By the way, at this point your prospect may begin to see you as something of a trusted advisor — you've obviously done some homework and are more than just another sales person in their doorway.

Questions to ask:

1. "What do you think this situation is costing?"

2. "How long has this been going on?"

3. "Where would you like this number to be?"

4. "I found this number in this trade magazine or study. Do you think it's close to what you're seeing here?"

5. "I did a quick estimate, can we take a look at it together?"

Many times it takes a number to make a situation real. **Find, agree, and track that number, for all specific solutions, throughout the sales dialog.**

8 BRAINSTORM THE NEGATIVES

Almost every solution with a real impact for your prospect will also create at least a couple of negative ripple effects. Finding them during your sales dialog is a huge win-win.

It's a win for the prospect as they avoid future problems while demonstrating they've done more than the usual due diligence as a purchaser. It's a win for you as well, as the prospect has allowed you to move around to their side of the table. You're now more than a salesperson just wanting them to buy something, you're a salesperson who's looking out for them.

A negative effect from a solution might look like this:

1. Improving efficiency in one operation might stress the next one or increase the total work-in-process (WIP) inventory in the system.

2. A software upgrade in one department might require the rewrite of software that pulls data for another department.

3. Centralizing (or decentralizing) a function may affect jobs at headquarters, regional, or local departments.

4. A change in delivery practices (such as implementing vendor-managed inventory) can disrupt accounts payable and quality assurance policies.

5. A cost reduction effort in one area may increase cost in another. For example, a change from 100% inspection of incoming materials to random sampling might require increasing the inspection rates somewhere else in the process. Or, a move to an easier to use customer order configurator may require restructuring of operations.

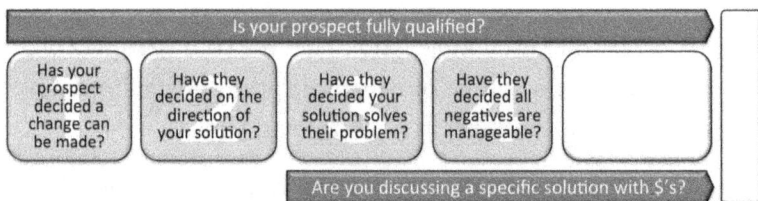

Is your prospect fully qualified?			
Has your prospect decided a change can be made?	Have they decided on the direction of your solution?	Have they decided your solution solves their problem?	Have they decided all negatives are manageable?

Are you discussing a specific solution with $'s?

A sure sign of a negative effect is, anytime your prospect begins a sentence with "Yes, but…" followed by something they don't want to happen. Listen for the "Yes, but…" statements. Here are a few examples:

- Yes, but doing this might crash our system.

- Yes, but this would require a lot of retraining.

- Yes, but our procedures don't support this workflow.

Make sure each negative the prospect has identified is vetted and solved to their satisfaction before moving ahead. For massive extra points, brainstorm and resolve potential negatives together!

Do not hesitate to bring in other resources from your own company to resolve a potential negative effect. This helps you solidify your role as a trusted advisor and resource.

On the other hand, discuss carefully with your prospect how best to use resources from their own company. Asking too many difficult questions of the wrong people at the wrong time can spin a sale off track.

Some of the questions you might ask include:

1. "How would this change affect up or downstream functions?"

2. "How is data shared right now? What would have to change?"

3. "Would this change affect your customers or your suppliers?"

4. "Would doing this automatically improve anything or everything else?"

Negative effects are the consultative closer's friend. Finding them and solving them is an incredibly positive closing stage.

9 ASK, YES ASK, FOR OBSTACLES

In the previous stage of the sales dialog, you and your prospect brainstormed potential negative effects, now ask the prospect to identify the obstacles to implementing your solution and then suggest ways to overcome each of those obstacles.

Let them take more of the lead here, but have a list of potential obstacles ready. Believe it or not, discussing obstacles at this point will advance the sale and secure your role as a trusted peer and advisor.

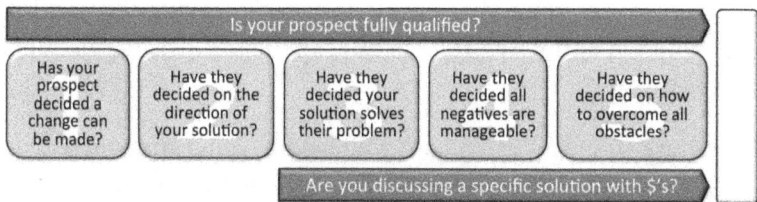

Is your prospect fully qualified?				
Has your prospect decided a change can be made?	Have they decided on the direction of your solution?	Have they decided your solution solves their problem?	Have they decided all negatives are manageable?	Have they decided on how to overcome all obstacles?
		Are you discussing a specific solution with $'s?		

Your goal in discussing obstacles is twofold: First, to find and resolve all the things that could affect the success of your solution. Second, you're bringing your prospect to the last small decision you'll want them to make: when to start.

Some of the questions you might ask include:

1. Are there existing activities that would need to be rescheduled or even reassessed?

2. Who would we need to coordinate with?

3. What security clearances will be needed?

4. Who knows the interface protocols?

5. What kind of other messaging would be needed?

6. What will the internal paperwork look like? (This may have been discussed at some point as you qualified the prospect.)

Listen carefully — is the prospect focused on what has to be overcome for a successful implementation of the solution? This is the inflection point I mentioned in the introduction: Is the prospect actively finding ways to overcome obstacles?

Put another way, is the prospect saying, "Yes, but…" followed by something negative or "Yes, but…" and then identifying an obstacle and describing a way to overcome it? The difference can be subtle but it's easy to hear, and with practice you'll even be able to suppress the smile you'll have when you hear your prospect overcoming obstacle after obstacle, paving the way for your solution and very often, in my experience, closing the sale themselves.

If they are still in "Yes, but…" followed by a negative then you'll need to back up a step or two. Usually the prospect hasn't really decided that the solution solves their problem, that the value is there, or that they don't truly feel that all likely negative effects can be managed. Back up and recheck that these decisions are firm. If the decisions are firm, then the prospect needs to be thoroughly re-qualified for Money, Authority, and Need, as something has changed.

Take notes, as the prospect is now actively identifying many of the implementation milestones for you and even the tasks and tactics needed to achieve them.

If they are engaged in this process, help them with those negatives before moving on to implementation obstacles.

Be prepared to "prime the pump" by asking about the use of your solution from their end back through the implementation of the solution, and then all the way back through the purchase process.

Working backwards (pulling) from a happy user back to the present state is much faster and more satisfying to the prospect than identifying ways to push something through their system.

Once they've made the relatively small decision, or series of small decisions, on how to overcome obstacles, they have all but closed themselves.

If your prospect resists taking that last step, remember to back up: A previous decision is no longer valid or your prospect is no longer qualified. It's the sales version of "rework."

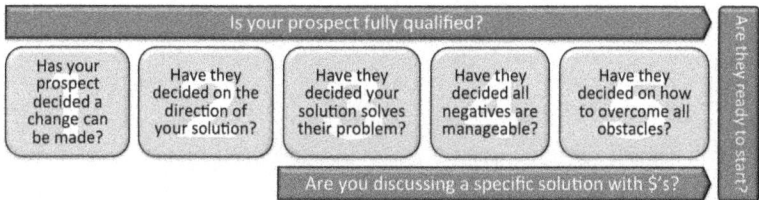

Is your prospect fully qualified?					Are they ready to start?
Has your prospect decided a change can be made?	Have they decided on the direction of your solution?	Have they decided your solution solves their problem?	Have they decided all negatives are manageable?	Have they decided on how to overcome all obstacles?	
		Are you discussing a specific solution with $'s?			

Most of the time they will ask you first, but if they don't, ask them "when do we start?"

It's one more small decision and, at this point, an easy one to make. And that is the perfect consultative close.

10 CONCLUSION

It is often said that the purpose of a company is to find and serve a market. Similarly, the consultative salesperson's purpose is to discover and meet a prospect's needs. The sales dialog described in this book is designed to help a salesperson do just that while moving a prospect to a decision. I call it a "respectful, but relentless" closing dialog.

A sequence of small decision stages serve as the backbone of this dialog. These stages exist only in the context of: 1) a qualified prospect, for 2) a specific solution of known value, until 3) they are closed. These are the states of the dialog. Without the first two states firmly in place, saying a prospect has made the decision required for a given stage really doesn't mean much. For example, we may have "Presented" but the prospect may not have even decided they can make a change in their situation. We may be "Overcoming Objectives" with someone who was qualified for a deal that is no longer under consideration.

We've all heard the ABC motto for sales: "Always Be Closing"– certainly no one has said it more emphatically than Alex Baldwin's character in *Glengarry, Glen Ross*. But nothing is more irritating to experience as a prospect than a salesperson who continues asking and asking for an order.

It would be both more clear and useful in consultative selling if we were to tweak ABC a tiny bit to ABCD, "Always Be in a Closing Dialog." Particularly thinking about how each action we take as a salesperson either advances the close or identifies where a prospect is on making a decision.

A final thought (and a warning):

Throughout this book, my constant theme has been that consultative selling benefits from a special kind of focused dialog with the prospect. It's important to remember as we sell that a "dialog" is more than a mere conversation — it's the creation of shared meaning. The dialog presented here was designed to improve sales performance, yet this was done with one of the goals being to reveal opportunities for greater mutual value.

While shared meaning and mutual value are both key components of a great business relationship, another component is trust. Trust is built by the making and keeping of commitments.

Please consider this a warning. You work hard to win an order. However, after your prospect has become your customer or client they will be increasingly exposed to other parts of your organization. A big part of your role with a new client is to guarantee that all commitments are kept. Both those you made and those made by anyone in your company.

Facilitating the sales dialog described in this book will separate you from your competition as a consultative closer and help you transform your selling relationships.

As the quality of the dialog you nurture with your prospects improves, they will enjoy more value, with less problems, more quickly.

You, on the other hand, will win more often, for more money, and at higher margins.

DIAGRAM OF THE CLOSING DIALOG

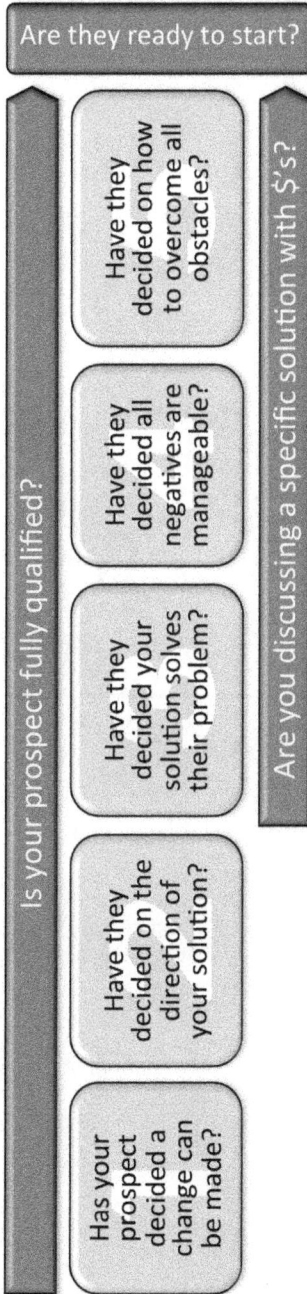

Are they ready to start?

Is your prospect fully qualified?

Are you discussing a specific solution with $'s?

Has your prospect decided a change can be made?

Have they decided on the direction of your solution?

Have they decided your solution solves their problem?

Have they decided all negatives are manageable?

Have they decided on how to overcome all obstacles?

ABOUT THE AUTHOR

Michael Clingan is an expert in sales innovation and strategic marketing. He calls his unique approach to dialog-based selling and creating innovative new market offers "Transformative Selling."

He has consulted with companies such as Abbott, Agilent, BioMed, British Telecom, College America, ITT, Materion, MEMC, Seagate, Tata, Thomson Financial, and TRW.

Michael's career includes global sales and marketing leadership roles in high tech, consumer electronics and professional services. His work with a blacklisted Nokia supplier resulted in that company becoming Nokia Americas Supplier of the Year — the case study on this work has been featured in numerous MBA programs.

Michael has a master's degree in experimental physics as well as a degree in English Literature. He is certified by both the Goldratt Institute and the TOC ICO.

He lives in Colorado, just outside of Rocky Mountain National Park, with his wife and their two daughters.

Close that Sale!

CLOSE THAT SALE!

Available for Keynotes and Workshops

- Your team will learn to create and advance a sales dialog until the order is closed

- They'll learn to diagnose a sale that's going poorly, how to fix it, and even when to walk away

- They'll learn to track and report real account progress and not just their last activity with a prospect

Attendee comments from Michael's presentations:

"Great presentation style. Funny, accessible. Helpful and succinct information that I can use today."

"This is by far the best presentation that I have been to at this conference. Michael is fantastic."

"Clingan is a great teacher who has vast knowledge in his area as well as a great sense of humor."

"Very helpful! The best presentation here!"

info@transformativeselling.com

Close that Sale!

TRANSFORMATIVE SELLING

Sales and Marketing Workshops

Each workshop is designed to help your team increase revenues and margins by:

- Developing effective strategies to expand markets
- Find and fix the real, and often hidden, constraints in your sales process
- "Look around corners." Anticipate new market opportunities
- Refocusing and thinking "customer back" and "around corners"

Perfect for offsites and retreats

info@transformativeselling.com